Miss Kelley

Hello,
Farm Animals

Written by Eileen Curran

Illustrated by June Goldsborough

Troll Associates

Library of Congress Cataloging in Publication Data

Curran, Eileen.
    Hello, farm animals.

    Summary: Depicts farm animals in their natural set-
tings doing their customary activities.
        1. Domestic animals—Juvenile literature.
[1. Domestic animals]   I. Goldsborough, June, ill.
II. Title.
SF75.5.C87   1985   636   84-8657
ISBN 0-8167-0345-0 (lib. bdg.)
ISBN 0-8167-0346-9 (pbk.)

Copyright © 1985 by Troll Associates, Mahwah, New Jersey
All rights reserved. No part of this book may be used
or reproduced in any manner whatsoever without written
permission from the publisher.
Printed in the United States of America

10 9 8 7 6 5 4 3 2 1

Cock-a-doodle-doo.

The rooster calls out to his friends.
"Hello, hello, hello!"
A happy day begins.

The farm animals are awake.

They leave the barn.

They go to the fields.

They go out in the sun.

The cows are hungry.

They eat the grass.

The pigs get dirty.

They play in the mud.

The hens are busy.

They lay the eggs.

Here are the chicks.

Soon they will grow.

The sheep and the goats

...are out in the sun.

And here are the horses.

How fast they run!

The farm animals are happy.

They eat and they play.

Soon they all go

...to the barn again.

Cock-a-doodle-doo.

The rooster calls out to his friends.

"Good night, friends!
Good night, good night!"

And the busy day ends.